Fact Finders®

WHAT WENT WRONG?

The Apollo 13 Mission

J. LEWIS CROZER LIBRARY
CHESTER, PA 19013

CORE EVENTS OF A CRISIS IN SPACE

by Kassandra Radomski

Consultant:
James H. Gerard
Education Specialist
NASA—Kennedy Space Center
Titusville, Florida

CAPSTONE PRESS
a capstone imprint

Fact Finders Books are published by Capstone Press,
1710 Roe Crest Drive, North Mankato, Minnesota 56003
www.capstonepub.com

Library of Congress Cataloging-in-Publication Data
Radomski, Kassandra.
  The Apollo 13 mission : core events of a crisis in space / by Kassandra Radomski.
    pages cm. — (Fact finders. What went wrong?)
  Includes bibliographical references and index.
  Summary: "Explains the Apollo 13 crisis, including its chronology, causes, and lasting effects"—Provided by publisher.
  ISBN 978-1-4765-4181-5 (library binding)
  ISBN 978-1-4765-5130-2 (paperback)
  ISBN 978-1-4765-5979-7 (eBook PDF)
1. Apollo 13 (Spacecraft)—Juvenile literature. 2. Project Apollo (U.S.)—Juvenile literature. 3. Space vehicle accidents—United States—Juvenile literature. I. Title. II. Title: Apollo Thirteen mission.
  TL789.8.U6A5775 2014
  629.45'4—dc23   2013023913

Editorial Credits
Jennifer Huston, editor; Bobbie Nuytten, designer; Wanda Winch, media researcher; Kathy McColley, production specialist

Photo Credits
AP Images: Eddie Worth, 21; CriaImages.com: John Robert Nash Collection, 9; Getty Images: MPI, 27, Space Frontiers, 23: NASA, cover (left), 5, 6, 11 (right), 17, 20, NASA: Johnson Space Center, cover (right), 4, 7, 16 (all), 19, 25 (top), 26, NASA: Spaceflight Center Collection, 12, 25 (bottom) 29; Shutterstock: art_design_ddh, blue mosaic design, echo3005, blue vector line art, eddtoro, 28 (left), Edwin Verin, 18, godrick, 28 (right), Igor Kovalchuk, space background, Jose Antonio Perez, 22, Kozhadub Sergei, circle frame

Primary source bibliography
Page 4, 6, 7, 8, and 17—NASA. "Apollo 13 Technical Air-to-Ground Voice Transcription." NASA: Johnson Space Center. www.jsc.nasa.gov/history/mission_trans/AS13_TEC.PDF.
Page 14—Jones, Tom. "Disaster at a Distant Moon." American Heritage, Fall 2008, 43–45.

Printed in the United States of America in Stevens Point, Wisconsin.
092013   007769WZS14

Table of Contents

CHAPTER 1
What Happened on *Apollo 13*?

"Houston, we've had a problem," astronaut Jim Lovell said on April 13, 1970. These chilling words were the first sign that the three astronauts aboard *Apollo 13* were in trouble. Until then, it seemed like just another mission to the moon.

Apollo 13's Mission

American astronauts had already landed on the moon twice the year before, so that part of the mission was routine. The crew of *Apollo 13* planned to land in the **Fra Mauro Highlands**, a rocky area on the moon with a giant **crater**. That part of the moon had never been explored, and **NASA** wanted to find out more about the crater. But the *Apollo 13* mission would make headlines for much more frightening reasons.

MISSION CONTROL

When astronauts are in space, they get guidance and information from the people who work in Mission Control in Houston, Texas. The scientists in Mission Control can tell if the spacecraft is on the right path. They also **monitor** the spacecraft for any problems. Mission Control's flight director makes all the final decisions. The astronauts are expected to do what Mission Control directs them to do.

(From left to right) Jim Lovell, Jack Swigert, and Fred Haise made up the crew of *Apollo 13*.

Meet the Crew

Astronauts Jim Lovell, Ken Mattingly, and Fred Haise were selected for this important mission. But about a week before the scheduled launch, the crew was exposed to **German measles**. Mattingly had never had the measles. NASA forbids astronauts to go into space if they are sick or might become sick. So Jack Swigert replaced Mattingly just three days before the launch.

Fra Mauro Highlands–a rocky area on the moon where a 50-mile- (80-kilometer-) wide crater is located

crater–a hole made when large pieces of rock crash into a planet or moon's surface

NASA–National Aeronautics and Space Administration, which runs the U.S. space program

monitor–to watch closely

German measles–a contagious illness that gives you a rash and a slight fever

"Houston, We've Had a Problem ... "

Despite the last-minute change in the crew, on April 11, 1970, *Apollo 13* launched from Kennedy Space Center in Florida. But about five minutes after liftoff, one of the five engines shut down earlier than it should have. After this **malfunction**, the mission ran smoothly for the next two days.

On the night of April 13, the astronauts filmed

"[The] spacecraft is in good shape as far as we're concerned," said the CapCom in Mission Control. "We're bored to tears down here."

themselves to give viewers a tour of the spacecraft. But none of the TV networks aired the program. They thought Americans were bored with space travel. It was mostly just the astronauts' families and a few workers who watched from a room at Mission Control.

Apollo 13's Saturn V rocket blasts off on April 11, 1970.

After the broadcast the **CapCom** asked Swigert to stir the liquid **oxygen** inside the oxygen tanks. Liquid oxygen fuels the spacecraft and helps the astronauts breathe. Swigert flipped a switch to stir the tanks, but something went terribly wrong. The crew heard a loud bang and felt the spacecraft shake. An alarm sounded and warning lights lit up, indicating a loss of power inside the spacecraft.

"OK … Houston, we've had a problem here," Swigert reported to Mission Control, according to NASA transcripts.

"This is Houston. Say again, please."

"Uh … Houston, we've had a problem," Lovell replied.

malfunction–a failure to work correctly

CapCom–short for Capsule Communication; these flight controllers are always astronauts

oxygen–a colorless gas in the air that people and animals need to breathe

From their headquarters in Texas, men in Mission Control watch the astronauts in space.

Mission Control didn't know what was happening on *Apollo 13*. Neither did the astronauts. There were so many problems occurring all at once that they couldn't believe what was happening. They thought there had to be some kind of mistake. The **gauges** showed one of the spacecraft's two oxygen tanks was completely empty, and the other was rapidly being drained. Two of the three **fuel cells** had also quit working. Alarms were buzzing, and warning lights were blinking. Astronauts train for problems in space, but they'd never trained for so many things to go wrong at once. Then Lovell looked out the window.

"We are venting something out into the—into space," he said to Mission Control.

What looked like misty fog was actually oxygen leaking out of the spacecraft. *Apollo 13* was more than 200,000 miles (321,869 km) from Earth, and the spacecraft was quickly losing electricity and oxygen. At that point everyone started to wonder if they'd still be able to land on the moon. But more important, would they make it back to Earth?

gauge–a dial or instrument used to measure something, such as an engine's temperature

fuel cell–a device that houses the main source of power on a spacecraft

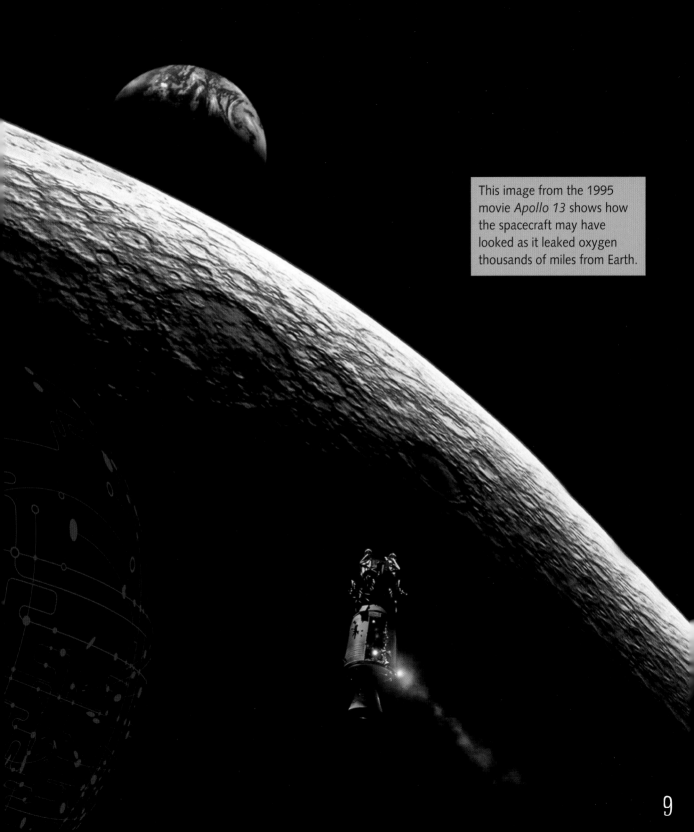

This image from the 1995 movie *Apollo 13* shows how the spacecraft may have looked as it leaked oxygen thousands of miles from Earth.

CHAPTER 2
Apollo 13's Problems Continue

The problems on *Apollo 13* continued to pile up. With no solution for the leaking oxygen, the flight director canceled the **lunar** landing. Instead the scientists in Mission Control turned their attention to getting the astronauts home safely.

First, the astronauts quickly moved into the lunar module. It had a separate supply of oxygen, battery power, and water. Then they shut off all power in the command module to save energy for the return to Earth. It was the only part of the spacecraft with a **heat shield**, so it had to be used for re-entry.

How to Get Home

Next they had to figure out *how* to get back to Earth. The quickest option would be to turn the spacecraft around and head back to Earth. This route would take only two days. But it required using an engine that was located near where the explosion had occurred. No one knew if this engine had been damaged in the blast. If it had been damaged, or if anything went wrong while firing it up, the spacecraft could fly straight into the moon.

DID YOU KNOW...?

Initially, Americans had little interest in what seemed to be an ordinary mission to the moon. But after news broke of the explosion on *Apollo 13*, viewers were glued to their TV sets watching news reports about the mission.

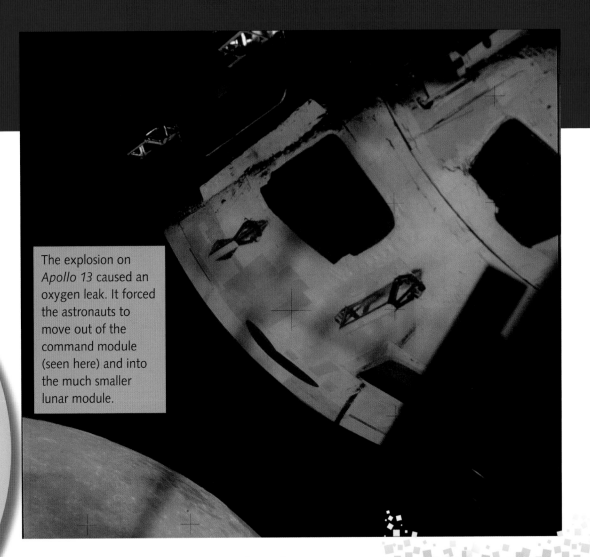

The explosion on *Apollo 13* caused an oxygen leak. It forced the astronauts to move out of the command module (seen here) and into the much smaller lunar module.

The other option worked like a boomerang. In this option *Apollo 13* would circle around the moon and use its **gravity** to pull the spacecraft back to Earth. This route would take four or five days, and the astronauts risked running out of oxygen, power, or water. It doesn't seem like it, but this option was safer. So the flight director decided on the longer trip around the moon.

lunar—having to do with the moon

heat shield—a covering that protects the spacecraft from extreme heat

gravity—a force that pulls objects with mass together

Life in the Lunar Module

The lunar module was made solely for landing on the moon. It was designed to hold only two astronauts for two days. But Lovell, Haise, and Swigert were forced to live in it for four days. With three men, it was pretty cramped. Also, to conserve energy, the astronauts turned off most of the power. They used just enough to stay alive and communicate with Mission Control. As a result, the lunar module soon became very cold—so cold that frost formed on the windows. The temperature dropped to about 38 degrees Fahrenheit (3 degrees Celsius)—as cold as the inside of a refrigerator!

It was so cold and uncomfortable that the men were unable to sleep for more than a few minutes at a time. Because of the living conditions in the lunar module, Haise got sick and developed a fever. He was tired, achy, and shivering. Despite his illness, Haise was determined to help the crew get back to Earth.

"I've been a lot colder before, but I've never been so cold for so long."
—Astronaut Fred Haise recalling his time in the lunar module

Just when they thought things couldn't get any worse, carbon dioxide started filling the lunar module. Carbon dioxide is an invisible gas that's released when people breathe. In the enclosed spacecraft, too much could be poisonous. The command module had a good **filtering** system that could get rid of the carbon dioxide produced by three men. But the lunar module's system was only made for two men. If something wasn't done quickly, the carbon dioxide level in the lunar module would become dangerously high. If it got too high, the astronauts would start to feel light-headed and sick, and eventually they would die.

DID YOU KNOW...?

For four days, the *Apollo 13* astronauts were forced to store their urine in plastic bags on the spacecraft. Urine is usually dumped overboard through a venting system. But once the *Apollo 13* astronauts were in the lunar module, they were told not to do that. If they did, the small force created when the urine emptied into space could change their flight path. No one wanted to take that risk.

filter—a device that cleans liquids or gases as they pass through it

Engineers in Mission Control came up with a solution to rising carbon dioxide levels in the lunar module. Then the astronauts had to make the same filtering system in space.

The engineers in Mission Control scrambled to come up with a solution. There were plenty of filters in the command module, but they were square, and the lunar module's filtering system was round. The engineers worked around the clock to create a hose to connect the lunar module to the command module's filtering system. Now the astronauts needed to create that same filtering system using materials already on the spacecraft.

Mission Control explained to the astronauts how to make the hose using cardboard, plastic bags, a hose from a space suit, and duct tape. But would it work in space?

Everyone watched the carbon dioxide level on the spacecraft. Little by little, the gauge went down. Within an hour the carbon dioxide levels in the lunar module were back to normal. Everyone breathed a sigh of relief.

Preparing for Re-entry

By April 17 *Apollo 13* was getting close to Earth. At this point the crew had to move back into the command module to prepare for re-entry into Earth's atmosphere. The astronauts then released the service module with its failed oxygen tanks. Lovell, Swigert, and Haise watched the service module float by them as it slowly drifted off into space. That's when they saw how badly it was damaged.

"There's one whole side of that [spacecraft] missing," Lovell called to Mission Control. The explosion from the oxygen tank was so powerful that it blew off the entire side of the service module. The men aboard *Apollo 13* were lucky to be alive. But they didn't have time to stop and think about it. They needed to prepare for re-entry.

A large portion of the service module blew off during the explosion on *Apollo 13*.

DID YOU KNOW...?

Before heading home, the astronauts also had to shed the lunar module, where they'd spent the majority of their journey. When they did, Swigert said, "She sure was a good ship."

As the spacecraft got closer to Earth, it was cruising at almost 25,000 miles (40,234 km) per hour. Compare that to a car traveling down a freeway at 65 miles (105 km) per hour!

When a lunar mission returns, the astronauts normally lose all contact with Mission Control for about four minutes. But this time four minutes passed, and there was no word from the astronauts. Three more minutes went by. Still no contact. Everyone in Mission Control was on edge. After all they'd been through, they wondered if something else had gone wrong.

Apollo 13 Timeline

April 11, 1970, 1:13 p.m. (CST): Launch of *Apollo 13*

April 11, 1970, 1:18 p.m.: The center engine shuts down two minutes earlier than planned.

April 13, 1970, 8:27–8:59 p.m.: The crew broadcasts live from *Apollo 13*.

April 13, 1970, 9:05 p.m.: Swigert flips the switch that stirs the oxygen tanks.

It wasn't just Mission Control that was on edge waiting to hear from the astronauts. The astronauts' families were waiting. People across the United States were watching on TV, waiting anxiously for word from the astronauts. Finally, just after noon central standard time (CST), they heard Swigert's voice. A few minutes later, the spacecraft appeared on TV with puffy clouds and a bright blue sky behind it. Then the parachutes opened and the capsule carrying the astronauts landed with a splash in the ocean. The astronauts were exhausted, but they were safely back to Earth.

April 13, 1970, 10:10 p.m.: The astronauts leave the command module and move into the lunar module.

April 17, 1970, 12:07 p.m.: The *Apollo 13* command module splashes down in the Pacific Ocean.

April 13, 1970, 9:08 p.m.: A loud bang is heard on *Apollo 13*. Lights and alarms go off. One oxygen tank is completely empty. The other tank is leaking oxygen. One fuel cell fails, then another.

April 13–17, 1970: The astronauts survive in the lunar module with limited power and water.

CHAPTER 3
Searching for a Cause

Following the safe return of the *Apollo 13* crew members, a team studied what caused the problems on the spacecraft. Team members discovered that the problems with Oxygen Tank 2 started long before *Apollo 13* blasted off. Oxygen Tank 2 was originally installed on *Apollo 10*, but it was taken out before the flight. When it was removed from *Apollo 10*, it was accidentally dropped. This damaged the inside of the tank, but no one knew. Also, during preflight tests for *Apollo 13*, the wires inside the oxygen tank were damaged. But again, no one knew.

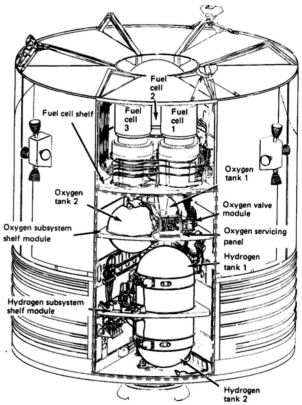

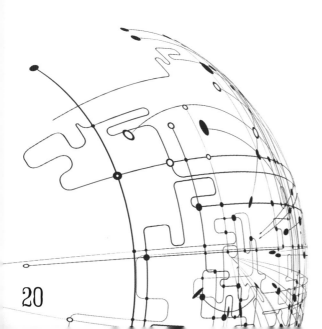

There were no obvious signs of problems with Oxygen Tank 2 until Swigert attempted to stir the oxygen tanks. In doing so, the wires that had been damaged during preflight tests started a fire inside the oxygen tank. The fire increased the pressure inside the tank, which caused it to explode.

The explosion in Oxygen Tank 2 damaged Oxygen Tank 1. Nearly all the oxygen stores needed to power the spacecraft were lost. What little power was left was saved for re-entry to Earth.

The crisis on *Apollo 13* made headlines across the world as these London newspapers show.

Changes to Future Space Travel

The problems on *Apollo 13* resulted in changes to later space travel. *Apollo 14* launched eight months after *Apollo 13*'s return. By then a third oxygen tank had been installed in the service module. *Apollo 14* successfully completed the mission that was originally assigned to *Apollo 13*.

Today *Apollo 13* is called a "successful failure." It did fail to achieve its goal of landing on the moon. But it was a success because the astronauts made it safely back to Earth despite numerous problems. In the end, that was the most important goal.

Was *Apollo 13* doomed before it took off because it was given the unlucky number 13? The astronauts and the men in Mission Control didn't believe so. In fact, the crew of *Apollo 13* say they were lucky to have survived after so many things went wrong.

The crew of *Apollo 13* made it safely back to Earth after six frightening days in space.

CHAPTER 4
Unlike Any Other Manned Mission

NASA had learned a lot about space travel since its first manned mission in 1961. Most of the missions were successful, even if minor problems occurred. Each mission had a goal—a task that the astronauts were supposed to complete. A mission was considered a success if the goal was accomplished. However, there were some missions where the astronauts failed to accomplish their goals. Other missions failed because the astronauts' lives were in danger.

Gemini 8, *Apollo 1*, and *Apollo 13* were all missions that failed to reach their intended goals. In comparison, all three missions experienced challenging, life-threatening problems. But in contrast, each problem was different.

Gemini 8

When *Gemini 8* launched on March 16, 1966, the crew's goal was to connect to another space vehicle. They achieved this goal, but then the spacecraft began spinning out of control. The spinning motion made it difficult for the astronauts to see clearly. Astronaut Neil Armstrong performed an emergency procedure that stopped the spinning. But it used up so much fuel that the astronauts were forced to make an emergency landing in the Pacific Ocean. Although the spinning motion made the astronauts dizzy and sick, they were not hurt, and they safely returned to Earth.

Astronauts Neil Armstrong and David R. Scott arrive safely after a successful mission aboard *Gemini 8*.

DID YOU KNOW...?

In 1969, Neil Armstrong became the commander of *Apollo 11*. He was the first man to set foot on the moon.

Apollo 1

The *Apollo 1* mission took a deadly turn on January 27, 1967. Its problems were different from those experienced on *Gemini 8* and *Apollo 13* because they didn't occur in space. *Apollo 1* was still on the launchpad when a fire broke out during a practice countdown.

The fire swirled through the spacecraft so quickly that astronauts Virgil "Gus" Grissom, Edward White, and Roger Chaffee were trapped inside. Those watching from the outside were unable to save them, and all three men died in the fire.

(From left to right) Virgil "Gus" Grissom, Edward White, and Roger Chaffee died when *Apollo 1* caught fire during a launchpad test, trapping them inside.

The *Apollo 1* spacecraft never made it off the launchpad. It caught fire during a practice exercise.

The crew of *Apollo 1* was performing a preflight test that went from routine to dangerous in seconds. *Apollo 13* also went from an ordinary mission to a life-threatening one in a short time. The difference between them was that the *Apollo 13* astronauts had time to figure out solutions to their problems. But most important, they survived.

	Mercury-Atlas 6 **February 20, 1962**	*Gemini 8* **March 16, 1966**	*Apollo 1* **Jan. 27, 1967**
Length of mission	Nearly 5 hours	10 hours, 41 minutes	Never got off the ground
Goal of mission	Send an American into **orbit**	First time one space vehicle connected with another	First scheduled launch of an *Apollo* spacecraft
What happened during the mission?	John Glenn became the first American to orbit Earth. Despite a warning light that the heat shield may be damaged, this flight was a success.	A problem caused the spacecraft to spin out of control.	Faulty wiring caused a fire, and the crew was trapped inside.
How did it end?	John Glenn returned to Earth safely.	The astronauts had to make an emergency landing, but neither of them was hurt.	All three astronauts died.

orbit–the path an object follows as it goes around the sun or a planet

Apollo 11 **July 16, 1969–July 24, 1969**	*Apollo 13* **April 11, 1970–April 17, 1970**
Eight days	Nearly six days
First time astronauts landed on the moon	Third attempt to land on the moon, this time on a rockier part of the moon
Despite an overloaded landing computer, Neil Armstrong and Buzz Aldrin landed on the moon with less than 30 seconds of fuel remaining!	Damaged oxygen tanks forced the astronauts to return to Earth before landing on the moon.
All three astronauts returned to Earth safely.	All three astronauts returned to Earth safely.

Astronaut Buzz Aldrin walks across the lunar surface on July 20, 1969.

Glossary

atmosphere (AT-muhss-fihr)—the layer of gases that surrounds some planets, dwarf planets, and moons

CapCom (KAP-kom)—short for Capsule Communication; these flight controllers are always astronauts

crater (KRAY-tuhr)—a hole made when large pieces of rock crash into a planet or moon's surface

filter (FIL-tuhr)—a device that cleans liquids or gases as they pass through it

Fra Mauro Highlands (FRAH MAHR-oh HYE-luhndz)—a rocky area on the moon where a 50-mile- (80-km-) wide crater is located

fuel cell (FYOOL SEL)—a device that houses the main source of power on a spacecraft

gauge (GAYJ)—a dial or instrument used to measure something, such as an engine's temperature

German measles (JER-man MEE-zuhlz)—a contagious illness that gives you a rash and a slight fever

gravity (GRAV-uh-tee)—a force that pulls objects with mass together

heat shield (HEET SHEELD)—a covering that protects the spacecraft from extreme heat

lunar (LOO-nur)—having to do with the moon

malfunction (mal-FUHNGK-shun)—a failure to work correctly

monitor (MON-uh-tur)—to watch closely

NASA—National Aeronautics and Space Administration, which runs the U.S. space program

orbit (OR-bit)—the path an object follows as it goes around the sun or a planet

oxygen (OK-suh-juhn)—a colorless gas in the air that people and animals need to breathe

Internet Sites

FactHound offers a safe, fun way to find Internet sites related to this book. All of the sites on FactHound have been researched by our staff.

Here's all you do:

Visit *www.facthound.com*

Type in this code: 9781476541815

Critical Thinking Using the Common Core

1. Look at the timeline on pages 18–19. Explain the importance of one of *Apollo 13*'s five engines shutting down two minutes earlier than expected. (Craft and Structure)

2. Describe the events that occurred on the night of April 13, 1970, which led to the *Apollo 13* astronauts having to move from the command module to the lunar module. (Key Ideas and Details)

3. What were the effects of the *Apollo 13* mission on future space travel? Think about the missions planned immediately after *Apollo 13* as well as missions planned far in the future. Support your response with research from both print and online sources. (Integration of Knowledge and Ideas)

Read More

Chaikin, Andrew. *Mission Control, This is Apollo: The Story of the First Voyages to the Moon*. New York: Viking, 2009.

Holden, Henry M. *Danger in Space: Surviving the Apollo 13 Disaster*. American Space Missions—Astronauts, Exploration, and Discovery. Berkeley Heights, N.J.: Enslow Publishers, 2013.

Oxlade, Chris, and David West. *The Apollo Missions and Other Adventures in Space*. New York: Rosen Central, 2012.

Woods, Michael, and Mary B. Woods. *Space Disasters*. Disasters Up Close. Minneapolis: Lerner Publishing Group, 2008.

Index

WITHDRAWAL